eBook Empire:
How To Create An eBook Empire on Kindle and Achieve Financial Freedom Forever!

by
Arthur Dylan

Table of Contents

(And what you will learn from this book)

Introduction
What this book is about and what it's not about. Why I started publishing eBooks — your motivations. How self-publishing changed everything. But I am an artist? — Discussing why people hold back from self-publishing and why they are wrong. Be a publisher, not just a writer.

1. Coming up with an idea for your book
Fiction or Non-fiction? Generating ideas. Reading and research. A tired old cliché returns. Stealing like an artist. Non-fiction vs Fiction. AdWords, pah! — Where we discuss using our intuition.

2. Ghostwriting
You can't build an empire all by yourself. How to find a good ghostwriter. Where to find a ghostwriter. What to ask for in your description. Trial and error. Why I like this platform, and why you should too.

3. Editing
Why editing is the most important process after writing. How to edit/ how to get someone to edit for you — DIY vs Lazy Way.

4. What to do when you have a finished book

A great title, not just a pretty name. Getting a cover — the Lazy Way vs DIY, a discussion. Your book description, a sales pitch, even for fiction. Using HTML. Categories — another important component of success. A free trick to sell more. Keywords.

5. Pricing and KDP

Piracy — how it's doing wonders for book sales. Pricing, my rules and advice for selling more with pricing. Having a perma-free book — The bait. How to make your book perma-free.

6. Building the Empire

The most important marketing technique, ever! What is a bundle and why should I? Rinse and repeat. Getting underwhelmed, a classic emotion of the newbie.

7. Marketing and other bits

Why I hate marketing. What you should do next, some valuable resources.

8. Things you shouldn't do

Discussing the term 'author platform'. Website and mailing lists discussed. My advice.

9. Multiple steams of income

How to turn your books into multiple streams of income. Other formats to sell your book.

Introduction

The method that I am outlining below in this book is one that I have used many times to create an eBook Empire. I've used many different names under many different genres.

This book is short for a reason. It contains no fluff, waffle or filler because I can't stand reading waffle, so why should you? I've intended for it to be easily read in a day or less. Any more would be a waste of everyone's time.

I am now sharing the tips I have accrued via trial and error over many years to create an eBook Empire. Here be my secrets…

What this book is about and what it's not about

What this book is about

This book is about how to create a huge eBook Empire on Amazon's marketplace. It's about how to come up with great idea's. It's about how to find a great ghostwriter, or ghostwriters, who can write for you, how to use them, how much to pay, what to look for and how to build great relationships with your staff.

This is about removing the time constraints put on most writers and argues that self-publishers (us) should think of ourselves as publishers, not just writers.

It's about how to price your book and why. About, how to maximise certain techniques to lure people into your series and have them fans for life.

It's about what to do when you've published your first book and haven't a clue what to do next...

What it's not about

It's not about how to write a book. If that's what you were after, put it down and go read something else — there's plenty of great books about how to write a book, some of them detailed at the back of this one.

It also doesn't go into the intricacies of things like building a cover, book descriptions and uploading to KDP, although I do address these.

It's not about building an author platform or any of that nonsense, in fact, it's very anti-building a blog and all that other time-wasting stuff.

Me and You

If you want to make money on Kindle and don't believe in get-rich-quick schemes, are prepared to put some time and effort into practice, and put your money where your mouth is — then you can come out of this with a very nice monthly income in a relatively short space of time.

I used to have so many different rubbish jobs and used to loath getting up in the morning because none of them were what I wanted to do. I was a chef, a pot washer, I worked for mobile phone company, in a shop, an office temp, a cinema… on and on and on, but with every new job I thought things would change, that they would get better. But they didn't — I had to find a way of making money for myself without working 'for the man'.

I never liked working for someone else. Knowing exactly

how much I'd make each month, while comfortable, it was torture for me. I mean, there's nothing to work for then is there? And I've always been a very creative person. The time I spent at work and not working on my own projects led me to despise work — I mean, I was just working on minimum wage, to make money for the guy at the top. I needed to find another way.

So I began a search and found out there was a way… I, like many others was drawn into the internet marketing world, until I found it soulless and vacuous. Then, after a year of searching, I discovered the blossoming new world of Kindle. I'd always written books and was trying to get one published myself, one that had taken me six years to write. So, I bought and read all I could about Kindle. Then over the last few years I've boiled the processes down into easy-to-follow-formulas, because that's what they are. A formula is something that has all the fluff removed, all the nonsense gone, and is just the core essence. Like anything, you will have to add your own DNA to the Kindle book world, just like I did.

I started writing on Kindle because I didn't want to go work anymore. I wanted to work for myself and now, I can finally say that I am there. Living the dream.

If this sound like you, then roll up your sleeves, make a cup of tea, get your note book and pen out, and sit comfortably.

How self-publishing changed everything

Amazon has changed everything. Prior to the Kindle eBook revolution, becoming a published author was a minefield.

You'd have to, and still have to now, spend lots of money printing out twenty or thirty copies of the first three chapters of your book, followed by cover letters, envelopes, postage and whatever else. And how much does that all cost? To then receive thirty rejection letters, and some never even reply. That's rude, isn't it?

And even if you were lucky enough to be picked out, often by some kind of lottery it seems, and your book was published, how much would you make? Well, look what you're up against — millions of books in book shops. It's another lottery altogether to actually sell any copies. It doesn't matter if it's good or not, if it doesn't have lady luck behind it, it'll be pulped before you can blink. And don't get me started on the time frame, sometimes it can take years, (years!) Until the book is published. In that time, you could've written many, many books for publication on Kindle.

We are living in a time of unbelievable opportunity. In the last ten years the opportunities for creating wealth in the digital revolution are, well, crazy. Think about it for a second:

— Apple's app store has enabled ordinary people to sit at home, create awesome apps that people love and sell them, creating overnight millionaires.

— Youtube has created an environment for people to become film stars in their own living rooms — virtual film stars where you can create a short film and upload it in seconds. The "You-tubers" then receive a cut of advert money from Youtube, and this has created full time You-tubers who live very comfortably from this money.

— And finally, Amazon, where people can write a book and publish it in minutes. Where there are no barriers, no gatekeepers from keeping you and your fans separated.

It's no surprise to me then that there are now more millionaires in the world than ever before. And get this, Amazon is the 11th most visited website in the WORLD. None of this would be possible without the internet. So, let's all bow down and count our lucky stars.

But let's just zap back in time, to how we would have had to achieve these riches in a previous world:

— Apps and software was always for the geeks, thousands of hours of work and knowledge was required to build software on large, slow, clunky machines. And no way of uploading it to the cloud — heaven forbid if you lost the floppy disc!

— To become a famous film star you'd have to have an agent, star in a string of Hollywood films.

— And, to write a book, well, we've been through that.

The earning potential — or, what used to keep me writing

At first it was really hard writing for Kindle. I set myself targets and missed them constantly. But then I read about the earning potential for Kindle and realised something…

What was annoying me was this: I had uploaded my first book to Kindle, a fantasy fiction for young adults, it barely sold. I used the KDP 5 free days and got 1,200 downloads. Brilliant! But after that? Nothing. Barely a few sales a week. That was frustrating, after all that hard work, it didn't feel worth it.

I read that you needed to have more books on Amazon to be successful, just having one wouldn't sell you many books. It said that you need to think long term. If you have one book out and you're making perhaps $200 a month, well think about this... think about how much you'll make a month, with TEN books out.

Aha! Eureka.

Let me repeat that again, if you're making a measly $200 a month with ONE book, Now imagine how much you'll make with TEN. Excited yet?

How this book pays for itself

How much did you pay for this book? The same price as a cup of awful Starbucks coffee? Right, good. We are agreed. And how much can you make by following my advice? Basically the answer is: unlimited.

It is down to you and your hard work, guile, your desire to learn and adapt, to learn from your mistakes and to never give up, that will make you your Empire. Just like I did. And I never have to go to work again.

So for a couple of dollars or pounds or whatever, you will learn the process, the formula that will make you much more over time. Even by selling one book that you publish, you will make the cost back of this book. Sweet, huh?

But I am an artist?

Some people said to me that they didn't like the thought of publishing on Kindle because it wasn't artistic — in their minds the version of the starving artist played loud and clear. They envisioned the slog of getting their book into print after many years, and living on the poverty line before suddenly becoming world famous and a millionaire overnight.

Yes, that's happened before *cough* J.K Rowling. But, as is often said, how many times has that happened? And also, it's an illusion, a myth, a fallacy that people tell themselves to feel better. They are just plying themselves with excuses so they can be lazy and do nothing. I consider myself an artist, for I create art. But successful artists are those who manage to make a living out of it.

And I actually also consider self-publishing to be much more artistic than traditional publishing. What can be more artistic than bypassing the gatekeepers and doing it yourself? You're forging your own path instead of following the well groomed dusty path towards traditional publishing.

Another myth…

"Isn't ghostwriting about getting hack writers to write a hack story?"

Errr… no. Again, I think some people just sit at home thinking this stuff up, so it gives them an excuse not to try anything new.

I've worked with some immensely talented people and that's what they are — people. They are writers that work for you (they are not ghosts either, obviously), they are talented and well-informed writers that will write whatever you want; fiction, non-fiction, humour, self-help, crime drama, whatever you like, there will be an expert writer on the subject who will make a better job of writing that book than you will. Why? Because they already have knowledge of it, which can be found in their description or bio.

Let me say this, these people are not hacks, many of them have their own published eBooks on Kindle and make a tidy sum by writing for others.

And again, this is foolproof, if you do hire a hack writer and they send you some garbled nonsense, then they won't get paid. Simple. Give them a one star and move on.

Be a publisher, not just a writer

This book you are reading here, is going to tell you that you must put on your publisher's hat. Once you've finished writing, you must turn into publisher mode. Because that's what you're doing, you're publishing your own work on Amazon, backing it with your own money in the hope that you turn a profit. Let me tell you, with my methods, you won't need to hope!

Being a publisher and getting into that mindset is as rewarding as writing. You get to learn lots of new skills that build up your base knowledge of self-publishing as a whole. It took me months to publish my first book, from formatting and editing, getting a cover made and all the other stuff. But now, I have a well-oiled system that can have it all done in a matter of days.

So, let's jump straight into it with our first topic:

1.

Coming up with an idea for your book

Right, let's get going!

If you want to build your empire, you have to start with an idea. And to write, or get a book written, you're going to need a great idea.

If you really want to publish on Kindle but you have no idea what your book or books could be about then start now by looking on your Kindle, or Kindle app.

Scan through your books on your bookshelf and answer these questions:

— Is it mostly fiction, or non-fiction?

If Fiction:

— Is it mostly thriller? Humour? Fantasy?

— What is the age range? (It's ok to read children's fantasy stories if you're an adult. I do!)

— What are the themes you are most interested in? Narrow it down, i.e a Magic fantasy would be Harry Potter, whereas an Epic fantasy would be Lord of the Rings.

If Non-fiction:

— What are they about? Fitness, food, volcanoes?

Trains?

— What are the themes? Informational books, or how-to books?

Other questions to ask yourself:

What is your day job?

What interests you the most?

What are your hobbies?

This is about finding out what you are passionate about and making a book about it. Don't think about what you can write that will make the most money, that's what hacks do, and they always fail. For me, I love writing and publishing and I've read just about every book about self-publishing. So I write about that.

Now, I hope you've started to make a list. If not, grab some paper and a nice pen and begin jotting stuff down on paper. Any ideas, just get it out. Don't edit yourself, just vomit all over that paper. Gradually whittle down the ideas into some basic idea for a book, or lots of books and pat yourself on the back. This should take anywhere between a few hours and few days.

Sometimes, it's better to take your time and let everything filter down through your subconscious, that, very often will provide the right answer after a couple of days.

Another tip: don't go on Google typing things like *"what should I write about"* or *"great ideas for books on Amazon"* or whatever. Don't be lazy!

Reading

Part of your research now that you have your basic ideas is to read through all the books you have on your Kindle or e-reading device. That's it, settle down in your sofa or bed and read.

Read everything that you have on the subject that you want to write about. And don't forget your notebook and pen! You should be scanning the table of contents, noting down anything that could be of use in your own book. Then reading and scanning through those books, taking notes down onto that paper for every thought that occurs to you. And believe me, if you do it right, you will get a lot. Expect that paper to be full before you even attempt to end the session.

For fiction writers, please go to your bookshelf or Kindle device and read the blurbs of those books and scan your favourites. Write down what you like about them, even if it seems pointless. Your mind will make connections under the surface. Maybe a name pops up that you like, or an idea, or some dialogue, or just the way it's set out or written. Whatever it is, WRITE IT DOWN.

Don't underestimate sitting down and just reading.

An old cliché

Here comes the old cliché — *don't reinvent the wheel.* There, said it. Phew.

When it comes to non-fiction, a lot of people talk about finding a niche. Now, what is finding a niche?

A niche is something that makes your book more sellable

and easier to write. Say you want to write a book about dogs. It's going to pretty long if you just jump into that straight away, right? And, how many other books are there out there about dogs? No, you have to refine and slim down that idea. So, you need to explore what is it specifically about dogs that you want to write about.

But you also need to make sure that the niche you want to write for has enough sales in it to make it worthwhile. You can check this by searching for your term on Amazon (on the Kindle Store), so "dog walking" say, then find one that most resembles what yours will be about. Click on it. Halfway down you'll see the categories that the book has been placed in, they look like this:

#15 in <u>Kindle Store</u> > <u>Books</u> > <u>Home & Garden</u> > <u>Animal Care & Pets</u> > **<u>Dogs</u>**

So click on "dogs" at the end of that category. Now a whole list comes up in order of the best books in that category from 1-100.

Click on the first and tenth books. Halfway down the page below the book description, it will say "Product description", in the same place where the categories were there will be this:

Amazon Bestsellers Rank: #2,835 Paid in Kindle Store (<u>See Top 100 Paid in Kindle Store</u>)

We are checking for that number, the 2,835. That's the important bit, note them down for the first, tenth and twentieth on the page.

If the first book has a rank of 10,000 or lower, as in

12,000, 15,000 etc, then that book is not selling much. If it's higher than 10,000, so 5,000 or 2,000 then go on and check the tenth and twentieth books. If the twentieth is around the 100,000 ranking, then you have a great chance of ranking in the top 20 on that category.

But this does not mean looking too far into it and finding some tiny niche, let's say for example you're looking at writing a book about walking dogs, and you see a niche that no one had written a book about; "Walking a dog at night in the forest." While you may think that's a great niche that no one else has written a book about and you think this will make you thousands, the simple matter of fact is that no one is going to buy that. Sorry, but who would?

But this is what you do:

Just copy what is already working. What I mean by this is — search the Amazon Kindle store for books that you want to write, say self-publishing, and research the many listings. How many are there? What are they about? Is it worth writing about this? You may think, as I did, that there are already loads of books on that subject, the market is flooded as they say. Well yes, but if you have a burning desire to really write something amazing then people will buy it, trust me. It may seem slightly contrary advice this one, but it's really about feeling the right idea out.

As they say nowadays: *"Steal like an artist"* (everyone does), Great advice — have a look at what's working and do your own version.

"It's not where you take things from—it's where you take them to." — Jean-Luc Godard

Non-fiction vs Fiction

So you can't decide if you want to write fiction or non-fiction. No worries, here is a list of the pro's and con's of both. Hec, even if you have decided already you can always change your mind. Some of the best storytellers I've ever known started by writing informational books.

Here's a little chance for me to have a moan: non-fiction on the Kindle store sometimes seems to be dominated by people who have jumped over to Kindle from the internet marketing bandwagon. You know that god-awful thing where people try and sell you information via pop-ups for $97? Trust me, I've bought some of them and they are horrible, usually crammed together packs of rubbish.

Where there is a great opportunity for wealth, you will see many desperate individuals clawing at the door with cheap, crass, badly made books thinking this is their ticket to the big time. Well, they are in for a shock. Thankfully, Amazon's algorithms kind of makes those cheap books invisible. But there are still a lot of informational books that are simply crap and they mysteriously have lots of great reviews. Frankly, these are the minority, but as someone with OCD, these annoy me the same as a patch of dirt would on the carpet.

This is your chance to write something great, get a great cover and put QUALITY out there into the world, not something that you think will make you a quick buck — if you are thinking that, then put this book down and search google for quick money making ideas. This is not that place, in fact, anything like that leaves me cold.

As to the pros of writing non-fiction, they sell a lot better on Amazon because people are searching for solutions to their problems and an eBook is a tight piece of information with bits they can jump straight to, rather than trawling through google to find their answers. They are relatively easy to write or outsource and don't need to be long. In fact, it's essential that you make it short — between 10,000 and 20,000 words is perfect.

The cons of writing non-fiction are that if you know nothing about a certain subject, it will come across as such. You will look like an idiot. You will get bad reviews and no one will buy it ever. If this does happen, I have a solution. What you do, simply, is remove it from Amazon, you send it to an outsourcer to re-write it with good quality information, get a new cover, and change the title. Re-upload and see what happens.

Also, it can be hard to find a good outsourcer who actually knows about their subject in depth. This isn't a problem, as you can learn and do anything if you put your mind to it. If you really want to write that book about snails then do it. But a bit of searching for the right ghostwriter can do wonders.

Writing fiction is even harder than non-fiction, but for some it comes more naturally. Inventing characters and worlds can be easy for some while torture for others, it all depends on who you are. The pros to writing fiction are that it's a great achievement when you have written something and put it out into the world. And it's fun!

The cons are that it takes a lot longer to write than a non-fiction, but it can be a hell of a lot more fun. Who doesn't like stories? Writing them can be both tiring, mentally exhausting and challenging, but the rewards are great. When you get people emailing you to say how much they loved your book and characters, that's when you know it's worth it.

AdWords, pah!

Lot's of books out there actually suggest using Google AdWords to find a great niche to write your book for. But is that really necessary?

Part of me thinks that it's just an excuse to fill up a chapter. A lot of these 'techniques' waste your time when you could be writing or outsourcing your next book. I've read about using it, but just always thought: *"What's the point?"* I even tried it, but again did not see the point. It's boring, pointless and takes away from a lot of the intuition that you need to build up. Yes, I said it, *intuition*. It's not some new-age thing, it's that gut feeling in your stomach that tells you the right thing to do.

This gut feeling or *Spidey-sense* as it sometimes known, comes about like this: you research a specific topic, the more you read, research and think about that topic, usually something you're interested in like a hobby, then all that research goes straight into your subconscious. This remembers everything. It processes everything you see, hear, smell, taste, touch. And once you learn enough about a subject, your subconscious will send you little messages, because it can work at the speed of light, making connections faster than your conscious brain can. That's why sportsmen often play on instinct, if they think too much it won't work. They practice for thousands of hours to become the best, until it becomes purely instinct. It's like driving a car or riding a bike. It's really hard at first, but after practice it sinks into our subconscious and we become naturals.

Instinct is that. The gut feeling that comes with knowledge. So forget about Google AdWords please, and rely upon your instinct, it's a lot more rewarding.

If you wanted a book to tell you the intricacies of using Google AdWords for finding a niche, then go buy another book that will tell you. But let me just say, this is my book, I am writing from experience, which means I cannot write about AdWords as I have never used it, didn't need to, won't need to. All the information you need you can get from Amazon.

So, forget numbers and stats, how many clicks did this and who searched for what, forget it. It doesn't matter. What matters is your ability to be able to come up with a great book that people will buy. Did they have Google AdWords a hundred years ago? No, not even 15 years ago, yet Stephen King and J.K. Rowling still managed to come up with great ideas that people wanted to read. Instead of searching for terms that people are searching for and thus making a book for them, come up with great book ideas and people will come to you.

If you just wanted to learn how to write your Kindle book and don't want to employ ghostwriters, then my next book out will detail how to write a book as quickly as possible while maintaining quality.

Arthur Dylan

2.

Ghostwriting

Now, we're here at last, the juicy bit of the book: Ghostwriting. It's a bad name really because it implies so many different connotations. The negative is when you hear about a celebrity autobiography that they obviously didn't write themselves, getting a ghostwriter to write it for them. That's not the ghostwriter's fault, and yes that's a hack of a book and clearly only written to make money.

They are also not ghosts. Obviously. A better name for a ghostwriter is a writer. They are talented, multi skilled and very knowledgeable. You can find a ghostwriter to write for you under pretty much any topic or genre.

What I am about to tell you are my most prized secrets. The reason I started to use ghostwriters wasn't because I couldn't write. It was because I didn't have enough time to write everything. I wanted to get all my ideas out there onto Kindle so I could build a name for myself. But the book I was writing was just too long and I was never going to get round to the other ideas. So I bit the bullet and went for it. Do I regret it? Not one bit.

It's easy getting a ghostwriter to work for you, they all tend to hang around the same places online. Which is handy. The only place I can recommend is oDesk, because that's the only one I use. There are others. A simple google search for outsourcing websites will bring up sites like <u>elance.com</u>, <u>iwriter.com</u>, and even <u>fiverr.com</u> at a stretch.

Now, I had a great idea for a children's horror series, a bit like the 90's Goosebumps series, that I wanted to write. I loved those books, so via nostalgia wanted to copy it. The problem was I already had three other books on the go. So after a bit of research and quite a few Kindle eBooks down, I went for it. I posted an ad for my eBook and explained the details of precisely what I wanted, I even requested that they come up with their own plot — for 20,000 words I offered $100. Ten applicants applied within ten minutes, after a few emails back and forth, I found the right guy and hired him that day. Simple, easy, fun, done. Now I felt like a productivity machine. I decided instead of being just a writer, I would be a publisher!

Let me say this, if you want to build a business, become a prolific author, or just get your books out there, then you need help. You cannot do it all on your own. I tried, it was exhausting and I failed, nearly giving up completely. So, use the help available — if you're worried about spending that much money, sort through your finances, sell some stuff, and wait until the end of this chapter where I explain how you should be excited by this, when I show you the numbers and potential earnings.

How to find a good ghostwriter

As I said, I use <u>odesk.com</u>. The following is a typical job posting that I would write. Feel free to copy it and put it into your own words.

This is in order, so if you are starting a new project on oDesk, bookmark this page and come back to it when you need to.

Firstly, make sure you select the right category. If you are doing fiction then select *"Writing & translation"* then *"Creative writing"* for example.

Give your project a title. If you're writing a horror children's series, then put something like: *"Ghost writer for fiction horror children's book series: _____ "* put the name of the series in the blank space.

Then describe the job, so something like this for fiction:

Hello all artists!

I am a writer myself with a number of books in print. But I need help in writing a new series called _____, which is based on the Goosebumps series for children from the 90's.

If you have good plot ideas, then let me know this in your application. Alternatively I can provide the plot and you just write.

1. *The genre is children's horror, thriller, chiller, scary, surreal and strange.*

2. *The characters must be endearing, no cardboard cut outs!*

3. *The stories need to be engaging and exciting with dramatic twists that the reader won't see coming.*

4. *The books target children, the main characters must be children*

5. *The plot can be written in first person, or third person. (you are the writer, your decision).*

6. *All the content will be thoroughly checked with Copyscape. Content must be 100% unique and original, written in clear, grammatically correct English.*

I am open to writers from all countries, providing your English, spelling, prose and grammar are top notch.

I am looking for long term relationships and as such the pay will be $100 for the finished book of 20,000 words or more.

However, if I like you and your work and want to commission more, then I will increase the payments for each book on a bonus scheme that I use for my other staff. If you are hardworking and loyal you could end up earning a very nice sum for each book!

Also, please be sure you are accurate and truthful about the job completion date. Job must be turned in as agreed upon. In the event of unexpected situations, kindly inform me in advance of the additional time required. Thank you.

Legal: this is a ghostwriting job and as such all ownership, copyright and claims to the material will be owned by me. I will retain 100% copyright of the work done and you may under no circumstance re-distribute or reuse the work.

Only native English speakers need apply.

Thank you and good luck!

Arthur

Now, there are a few important bits in this that I should explain. Offer to provide a plot, because sometimes the best writers can only write — this means you will just have to spend a little bit of time to come up with a cracking plot. If you can't do this, then again, just outsource it.

List the specific requirements for your book in bullet form. So list the genres, what the characters must be like. The 3rd bullet point is self-explanatory but you should still put it. The 4th, you must put your target audience. Then tell them if you want it in first person or third person.

The 6th is very important (although more for non-fiction) you must state that the content will be checked through copyscape.com, which is an online plagiarism checker. It doesn't cost much at all and it's pretty vital. If you publish plagiarised work, you will be kicked off Amazon!

Then, state who you would prefer to write it, from what country. Followed by an explanation of the money, I always state that if they are hardworking and loyal and we work together again, and they will receive more the next time. You have to dangle a carrot sometimes. Finally, you must state that the work will belong to you, you will own 100% of the copyright and can distribute the work however you please.

Sign off.

Next, input some tags so that people searching can find it, things like eBooks, storytelling, creative writing. These pop up anyway and most of the suggestions are correct.

Next, choose "Fixed price" and put in $100 or whatever you want. Followed by an End Date, you should give them between three and four weeks for a 20,000 word book. Don't be a taskmaster and request it back in a week, or they won't work with you for long.

Then select that the job can be found on Google. Then it asks if you want one freelancer, or many. I always choose just one. Next it asks if you want to upload a document, no point unless you have a plot for the book.

Next click on "Preferred qualifications". It opens out a set of boxes. In your project window you can also filter out certain people from applying. For instance, you can set it to only Native English speaking applicants, that way you won't have people whose second language is English and their writing comes across that way.

Then, you should put only four stars and up rating can apply, this means you will only get applicants who have a great response with their customers and have been rated 4 or 5 stars consistently.

Then tick the box that says "require a cover letter" — you want people to have to work for your job.

When you write your job description, it gives you a chance to write some questions at the bottom for them to answer. I'd encourage you to do so, write between two and three questions about why they want this project, what experience do they have?

And that's it. All done.

Unfortunately, I cannot recommend good ghostwriters for you, because they all write for different subjects. While I write books for children on horror, you might want a book about walking a dog. The same ghostwriter is unlikely to write about both, unless they are very talented.

Finding the right ghostwriter and sticking to them is

trial and error I am afraid. That's what I used and it worked. Yes, there were a few duff ones, but isn't there always? Just keep going until you find the right ones.

The reason I like oDesk is because it has a review system, a lot like Amazon, so you can filter out the time wasters and the newbies until you get the serious workers. You may have to pay a bit more, but what you get is quality. Just make sure you email them a couple of times to make sure they are the right candidate. If they come across well, then press that hire button, if not, don't bother.

3.

Editing

Now, editing is very important. You get your wonderful manuscript back from your ghostwriter and you're pleased as punch, do you upload it straight away to Amazon? No way. You need to put your reading glasses on.

Sometimes when we write, we cannot see a mistake if it jumps out in red squiggly underlines with arrows pointing from all around. We are blind to it. Ghostwriter can be the same. You must be the first editor. Some writers can be sloppy, their choice of words strange, their grammar wrong. Fresh eyes can be just what it needs. Make a copy of the document and start reading through.

Then, grab your mouse and keyboard and go through it again, removing anything that doesn't work, doesn't fit, and spell the misspelled words yourself. You can also add in anything you want to, that's the beauty of this, you can do that, this is your book now.

You don't want to put out a book with your name on that isn't edited well — believe me, if one thing will put off buyers quicker, it's that.

Now, if there are so many errors it's going to take you all year to edit, then send it back to them saying you're not happy about the state it arrived in. They should edit it themselves. Once this is completed, you have two options:

Leave it as it is and get it ready to publish. Or, pay an editor on oDesk, to edit the document quickly for say $20.

This is very important as an unedited eBook can get you more 1 stars on Amazon than anything else. They will forgive a bad cover, but bad spelling, grammar and writing? No way.

DIY vs Lazy Way

If you are strapped for cash, you can edit it yourself, or even send it to a friend. That is fine. Just make sure you check it with eagle eyes.

The beauty of Amazon is, if there are mistakes in there that you missed, you can always edit them out later and re-upload the book.

The lazy way is to pay someone to edit the entire document. So, you can use oDesk to do this and it can cost anywhere between $20 for a quick check up to $300 for a full check of everything, depending on how long it is. Also, there are some good editors who don't charge a lot on fiverr. com — but in my experience this can be hard to find.

If the ghostwriter you are employing is from another country, let's say you're from the US and you employ a UK writer, some of the spellings will be a little different. That's fine, just change them. No need to sack them.

4.

What to do when you have a finished book

KDP

https://kdp.amazon.com

When it comes to that glorious time when you have a finished book then it's time to begin by registering for Amazon's KDP. This is the place where you will upload your book and all its information. Get on there as soon as you can and familiarise yourself. It's not complicated, in fact it's easier than you'd think! But first we have a few more things to do:

A great title, not just a pretty name

So your book is edited and ready to go, what next? You may have thought that the title you already had was good enough? Maybe, maybe not.

A great title is not just a clever name, it must do a number of things: it must convey exactly what the book is about. If it's about self-publishing and the title for your book is *"grab a pencil"* then it just won't do. It must have *self-publishing* in the title, or at the very least the subtitle. Why? Because when people search for something on Amazon about self-publishing, they are not going to type in anything about a pencil. This is just an example, I know you won't be so stupid, but I do have people email me and ask *"why am I not selling any books?"* — their title is one of the things I point out.

If you have a great title that you want to use that is clever, funny and witty then use it. But you must employ the subtitle to your advantage. If it's about *self-publishing for cats*, then in your subtitle put *complete guide to self-publishing for cats*. Simple.

The title of your book is a keyword, a keyword that people search for when trying to find a book to buy. Sod artistry for a minute. You want to sell your book. You must make the title Amazon friendly. Amazon will pick your book out and place it on the list that the searcher made based on a number of things, the first is the title. Also, if the searcher sees your book and they've just searched for self-publishing, and your book doesn't convey a self-publishing vibe, then they will skip straight over it.

This goes for both fiction and non-fiction. With fiction, it's a little trickier, but I've managed it. If my book is about a teenage wizard say, then I have my title that is something like *"Freddy Underwood and the Magical Hamster"*, but then, in the subtitle, I use brackets and put (*"The Magic Teenage Wizard Series for Children"*) so, how many keywords are in there?

When someone types in *"magic teenage wizard"*, or even *"teenage wizard"* or any variation of these, then you will rank on page 1 of that search, all being well.

Getting a cover

This is a debatable subject. Many people out there say

you must pay for a cover. No questions asked. But the thing is, I made my first cover. I didn't want to pay $300 like my so-called guru book told me to. Neither did I want to pay $5 and get a crappy cover. I wanted quality. I didn't study art at school, nor Photoshop — so I spent a month and taught myself with Youtube videos and believe me, you can make great covers. It's the old argument of time vs money. Do you have the time to create great covers?

Ok, I'm going to lay down as many different ways of creating a cover as I can think of.

The Lazy Way

The first is by outsourcing it. This is the lazy way, for people who have the spare cash. The first place I'd recommend is *99designs*. I've heard a lot of good stuff about them, it costs upwards of $199, but if you don't like any of the designs people send in, you get your money back. Nice.

Next is fiverr.com, if you just want something cheap to start with then there are some great people on here who will do it for $5. It might pay to buy a couple and select the best one.

Lastly, it's oDesk again. You can find great graphic designers on here — the best thing to do is post a fixed price and see who bites. You don't want to spend a lot so put the bidding at $50 and see if you get anyone good. Remember, if you don't like it, you get your money back.

DIY

A great thing to purchase if you want to go DIY is the

CreativeIndie book kit. For $87, this course tells you how to create great book covers in Microsoft Word, of all things. Sounds like crap, it's really not. It's one of the best things I've done and the covers you can create are amazing. Well worth the money: Diybookcovers.com.

One of the things I do when going DIY are these:

If I have a fiction book for children and I want an illustration for my front cover then I go to: deviantart.com, fiverr.com, hireanillustrator.com, and search around for brilliant illustrators. Then I email ten of them and some will email back. Then, we have an email conversation and I tell them what I want. A good thing to do is send them a free copy of your book and see what images they get from it. Ask them to send some quick sketches of what they would do. Agree a price if you're happy with them, pay with Paypal, or Google Wallet and done! Keep them sweet, as if you have a series of books, or plan to have a series, then you want continuity with illustrations on the cover.

Next, I look for cool fonts that fit my genre. Just search for "free fonts" or "free fonts ____" and then a genre, like gothic in the space. Download these and try them out on Photoshop.

Put your author name on it. Make sure you shrink the picture down to thumbnail size, does it still read ok? If not, make the text bigger so it stands out.

If you have a non-fiction book, what I do is search for images on shutterstock.com, or fotalia.com and find a good one to use that sums up my book. So for self-publishing, I'd use a picture of some books, or a Kindle or something. Then place your fonts over the top in a new layer on Photoshop.

If in doubt, search Youtube for tutorials and follow the instructions. It may take more time than getting someone else to do it, but it's very rewarding when it works.

I will be writing another book purely about eBook covers at another time. So if you require more in-depth analysis, then wait around for that. Or search Amazon now for something more concrete if you're worried about creating the perfect cover.

Book description

Your book description is another big seller. You must describe your book shortly and succinctly.

If your book is fiction, then you must put:

The title of your book, followed by the subtitle underneath. Then, straight into the story. Don't mention more than three or four characters, otherwise the reader will get overloaded with information. Explain the main goal of the protagonist:

- Freddy is different because…
- And then one day something happens…
- And then he is thrust into a new world where…
- He meets…
- And they all go on a mission to save…
- But will they save her?
- Or will the evil ___ triumph?
- Read now to discover the mysteries in ____'s book.

You can then include below that a few reviews if you

have any, or you can make them up, I don't think it makes a difference. Just make sure the review sums your book up, it could be something like: "Harry Potter fans will love this!"

For non-fiction writers, small paragraphs work best, usually bullet pointed and alternating bold text if you can get HTML. You must tease, not tell. You must say what your book includes, but not the answers. You want them to buy it, not read the book description and know all the secrets. You must imply that by reading this book they will get all the secrets that they need to be successful, or a brilliant dog walker, or know what they need to know.

You have 4,000 characters to describe your book inside KDP. Don't use all of these 4,000 characters for goodness sake. When was the last time you read the entirety of a 4,000 character book description before deciding to part with a few bucks?

Writing the description is hard, I won't lie. It can take a full day to get it right. Again, you can outsource this. But you should persevere, it's a skill worthy of learning.

You should try and aim to get you book description plastered with a small amount of Amazon's very own HTML, which makes your text all lovely and visually appealing, not just a box of unreadable vomit. There are guides online for how to do this. Alternatively, just go on <u>fiverr.com</u>, someone will do it for $5.

Categories

The categories that you choose your book to be in can be slightly confusing for a newbie. I wouldn't worry too much as Amazon moves them around willy-nilly anyway. The best thing to do is this — choose your categories that you think best suit on your KDP page. Then after a few days email KDP customer service citing categories and ask to be placed in the categories you've researched.

Researched? Yes. Now okay, let's rewind. So before telling them what categories you want to be in, you must research. Go on the Kindle book store, search similar books to yours and see what categories they are in. It will be halfway down the page, near the rankings. It will read like this:

Kindle Store > *Books* > *Science Fiction & Fantasy* > *Fantasy* > *Sword & Sorcery*

Next, click on the category, so "sword and sorcery" — then click on the first and twentieth book on that page. What are their rankings? On this page, the first one is ranked #36 in the entire Kindle store, blimey. And the twentieth is #1,030.

Right, so forget that category. That's too hard. You'd have to be selling 20 a day to be up there.

Whereas in this category:

Kindle Store > Books > Teen & Young Adult > Science Fiction & Fantasy > Fantasy > Fairy Tales & Folklore

The twentieth book is ranked #31,480 and the first #31. So you could break the top 20 quite nicely.

It's a good idea to check the rank of the other books to see if you can break into the top ten. Find two categories that you can realistically actually rank in and email KDP asking to be put into these categories. This now means that people can find you by searching the categories on the left.

More sales!

Done.

Keywords

In your KDP page, you have the chance to put in seven keywords. These are what will make your book show up when people search in the Amazon search bar. So if you want people to find your self-publishing book about making e-covers, then type in phrases that you want your book to show up for. I would use: *self-publishing covers, how to create book covers, books about making covers…*

It may be helpful to get help on this one, a fiverr.com gig is perfect, they will do the research for you and find the best keywords. I've used this when keywords were not working.

TIP: This is a little bit cheeky, but oh well: I get a small group of keywords that I'd like to use and put them all together at the bottom of my book description. I just put this: "*tags: self-publishing covers, how to create book covers, books about making covers…*" and put as many as I can think of, but not too many otherwise it looks bad.

Piracy — how it's doing wonders for book sales

You may think that giving your book away for free is a stupid idea. You may also think that your stuff being pirated, that is, people downloading it for free online without your consent is a travesty? Am I right? Well, you're kind of right, it is rather upsetting, especially if you're a musician and can't afford to live, and everyone downloads your album you spent ten years creating, for free and you get nothing. That's annoying, but fortunately it's been found that stuff being pirated actually has a positive effect on book sales. Now that is a turn up!

Mr Neil Gaiman says that at first he was quite upset about his work being pirated on the web. However, it turned out to be a blessing in disguise as he started to realise that whenever his works were pirated, it actually helped his sales!

"Then I started to notice that two things that seemed much more significant. One of which was that places where I was being pirated -- particularly Russia (where people were translating my stuff into Russian and spreading it out into the world) I was selling more and more books. People were discovering me through being pirated. And then they were going out and buying the real books, and when a new book would come out in Russia it would sell more and more copies."

He persuaded his publisher to release a free copy of one of his books, *American Gods*, and sales went up 300%! He stumbled upon the fact that piracy is just the lending of books.

"That's really all this is. It's people lending books. And you can't look on that as a lost sale.... What you're actually doing is advertising. You're reaching more people. You're raising awareness. And understanding that gave me a whole new idea of the shape of copyright and what the web was doing. Because the biggest thing the web was doing is allowing people to hear things, allowing people to read things, allowing people to see things they might never have otherwise seen. And I think, basically, that's an incredibly good thing." *(Source: techdirt.com)*

5.

Pricing and KDP

Ahhh, pricing. The wonderful world of pricing our books for maximum dough.

Let's start with a little backstory. Prior to 1935, books were very expensive and could only be afforded by the well to do. They would be hardback and leather bound. As such, most people didn't and wouldn't read. However, a genius invention took over: the invention of the paperback. The man was Allen Lane, he wanted to make books affordable for everyone, and available in train stations alongside magazines. And for the same price as a pack of cigarettes. Lane's publisher turned down his idea of cheap paperbacks and so Lane funded the project himself, calling his firm Penguin.

"Lane's paperbacks were cheap. They cost two and a half pence, the same as ten cigarettes, the publisher touted. Volume was key to profitability; Penguin had to sell 17,000 copies of each book to break even."

This opened up the book world to millions of new readers — the idea had been tried before in the sixteenth century by a Venetian man called Aldus Manutius. He wrote what were dubbed "penny dreadfuls". They were lurid romances published in double columns — they did not catch on among the upper classes who considered them mightily trashy.

Let's zap back to now — just recently we had another evolution in the book market, the rise of self-publishing and digital books. The price of these digital books is very interesting. The difference in pricing with the advent of the paperback compared to a big hefty hardcover was significant, around 10% of the actual cost. Now, a paperback costs $10 or so. And the average price of a Kindle book is $2 — so the price has jumped back down by approximately 20% of the cost of a paperback. This has great potential for the poor who can now afford to read again, just like they did when the Penguin paperbacks came out — providing that they get themselves a Kindle that is. I can honestly say I've read more since the Kindle has come out.

If anything tries to stay as it is — that is to conserve — it will wither and die, just like the publishers who refused to turn their books into paperbacks. And just like the publishing houses that now despise everything about Amazon and refuse to make eBook copies. To remain current you must be flexible, in the flow, ready to adapt at any moment. Our world is changing that quickly.

History lesson over. To get maximum sales from your book, it must be priced correctly. These are my rules:

1. If you have a very short 5,000 — 10,000 word book then go for 99c — $1.99.

2. If you have a book that's longer than that, say 10,000 — 20,000 then I'd go for between $1.99 — $2.99

3. If you have a bigger book than that, say a fiction book of 50,000 — 80,000 words, then anything between $2.99 and $7.99 is good.

4. If you bundle all your books together, let's say all your fiction books and the word count is 100,000 plus, price it at $9.99 that's the maximum you can put it at to receive 70% royalties.

So what will you make on each book?

1. On a 99c sales, you make 35% royalties, so around 33c

2. On $1.99 you'd get 70c and for $2.99, $2! (That's the sweet spot for most people).

3. Anything between $2.99 and $7.99 is 70% royalties, so on $7.99 you're looking at $5.50

4. On the maximum of $9.99 you'll get $7

Where else in the book publishing world can you get *70%?!*

Some people talk about a pricing strategy of starting at 99c and then moving it up to $1.99 then $2.99 — I'd agree with this. Often when I'm not getting many sales on a particular book, I lower the price, make sure I tell them it's been lowered in the book description. Then I tend to see a bit of a pick up that carried over when I raise the price again.

Having a perma-free book — The bait

This is a little known trick that not many people employ and it works absolute wonders. I hope by now you have realised that to make serious dough on Amazon you must have lots of books out, quality and quantity, right?

Ok, a book series is the best way to do this because you lead people down a sales funnel (more on that later). Instead of writing some huge book about self-publishing, write ten small ones as part of a series — this will make you more money.

So, let's say we have five books out in a series, they are all priced well at 99c or 2.99. But not many people are buying them. You need to change things up — so this is what you do: you make the first book FREE, completely free forever, called perma-free. This then makes people see it, think "*Ah that's free I might as well download it*", they download it (lots of downloads for one book also pushes all your books up the rankings). Some people who download it, love it and want to read the next book. And oh look, there's the next book waiting for them, and it's only 99c or 2.99. You've just made a sale and it was easy. Instead of trying to convince them to buy the first, you've easily converted a sale for the second without any effort.

This is classic new age marketing — I first noticed it on the Apple App store with Angry Birds. I saw it up there and it was free so I thought why not, let's try it, can't hurt. I played it, loved it and wanted more! So I looked around and sure enough there was another one out, but guess what? It was 69p. Did I buy it, or did I think well 69p that sure is a lot? Did I hec, I went and bought it — well and truly into their sales funnel I went. They used a bait. Just like going fishing, if you want to lure customers into buying your books, you got to use a bait.

You can do what I did and write a book that I know I'm going to release as a perma-free, or you can go to your first book in the series, especially for fiction, and make it free. Simple, done and you will sell tons more books.

If you don't have any books out yet, don't worry, just remember this and come back to it when the time is right. Bookmark this page and stick a post-it note on your wall somewhere.

How to make your book perma-free

Here is how I did it, by following the instructions from this guy on Goodreads, website below:

Basically it involves using <u>smashwords.com</u> and uploading your book there and making it free. Amazon will price match it (eventually) and your book will be perma-free on Amazon. Easy.

Follow the instructions on this site:
(<u>https://www.goodreads.com/topic/show/1722676-making-your-ebook-perma-free-on-amazon</u>)

6.

Building the Empire

Make a series

Making a series is the number one thing you can do, more aimed at fiction than non-fiction, but the same principles apply. This is very important, like the last chapter I explained that you need to lead people into a sales funnel — if you only have one book then there is no way of doing that.

Why do you think Disney are making Toy Story 4? Because it's a perfect sales funnel, you watch Toy Story 1 and then see there's 2 more. What you are going to do, ignore them?

If Harry Potter only remained as 1 book, do you think J.K. Rowling would be as popular and rich as she is today? Doubt it.

Making a series is easier than you might imagine, although you still got to put the effort in. Here are some tips (this is mainly for fiction):

Plan a whole series at once as if you would plan a book. So plan what happens at the end of your series. Then start planning what happens in each book. That way you can drop breadcrumbs to future books and your fans will love it.

Keep all the covers basically the same, maybe change the

background colour and illustration. Keep the font of a series the same. That's a must. If all the covers look different then it's confusing.

Make sure people know what book is what, make the book number clear and visible. You don't want people moaning because they accidentally bought book 3 hoping it was book 2.

This is how I would price a series of 6 books:

1. FREE
2. 99c
3. 2.99
4. 2.99
5. 2.99
6. 2.99
7. BUNDLE: All the books together in one download for between 7.99 — 9.99. (This saves them between $3 — $5 and you get more royalties in one go)

The trick to making a series is to make interesting books about the same subjects. So with self-publishing you could have one book for beginners about how to put your book on Amazon, another talking about HTML for your book description, another about how to get reviews and another about how to write fast. That's four books already!

Also, another tip, if you want to write for fiction and non-fiction, use different names. Invent a pseudonym for either. People will get annoyed or confused if you use the same name for a dystopian fantasy and your book about how to walk a dog.

Rinse and repeat

Once that book is up there and published on Amazon, you should be planning your next book. Whether you are writing it or you're getting it ghostwritten. You should be planning. The problem is, so many people give up way before they should, they get turned off by something and they throw their dummy in the air and walk away. Persistence is the key.

As soon as that book is finished and on Amazon, start planning.

To build your Empire, you must keep going — imagine yourself as a factory. Certain things you must hire out, and other things must be automated and you have hired staff, but one thing is for sure… it keeps producing.

Getting Underwhelmed

You will feel blooming great when that first book goes live. The world spins in your quarter, and you go to bed at night dreaming of the untold millions that will be flooding into your bank account. Well, I'm afraid that isn't quite true. It takes a lot of hard work to get this far, so well done, however there is still much work to be done. I don't want to lie to you, it's hard work.

In fact, it's safe to say that when you upload your first book, you will get hardly any traction at all. If you list it as free then you will see lots of downloads and that's exciting, maybe a few sales after that but not much, barely pennies in royalties. So, what do you do to combat this? Walk away, say the self-publishing world is not for you? No, of course not! You roll your sleeves up and write book 2. That's the only way you will make money, by having book 2 out. And then book 3 and 4.

7.

Marketing and other bits

Time for a small confession. I absolutely hate marketing. It leaves me cold and I wake up shivering in a wet mess. Some people live for the marketing side and get some kind of kick out of it. Just depends of what kind of person you are. I was always raised on Bill Hicks and artsy types, so any kind of stuff like that leaves me feeling like I'm selling my soul. Anyway, that's why I use other techniques like offering a book for free and building a series that gets people to buy rather than shoving adverts down their throat. However, there are lots of marketing strategies that do work, that I've used — they are a necessary evil, if you want to get initial traction for your book.

This is my advice:

Once you've published your book, it can feel like you're at a loose end, you'll feel like you need to tell people about your book. So you blast out FaceBook and Twitter messages. Does it work? Pah, hardly.

— The first thing I would do is set up a KDP free giveaway. I would schedule it for in a few weeks until your book settles down into Amazon and maybe gets a few reviews under its belt. After those few weeks, all the relevant information should be available about your book on

Amazon's eco system.

— Secondly, I would go on fiverr.com and see what promos people are offering for $5. The best one's I've got are when people have specialised Kindle lists for free book lovers. I'd buy up a whole ton of them within my budget of say $50 and this would kick start the free downloads which will boost us up the Amazon rankings. Again, I cannot recommend great gigs as it changes so often that in a couple of weeks those links will be dead. There are even gigs on here that will submit your book to free sites across the internet. A great and handy resource!

With fiverr gigs it's a good idea to experiment and find what works for your, which gigs are good and which are pants. Try and correlate which ones got you the downloads so you can use them again.

— There are many other great sites which help with the promotion of your book, some are very hard to get onto but if you are one of the lucky ones then hooray!

Search for bookbub.com and pixelofink.com — it's unlikely you will get picked up by them immediately. They require a certain number of reviews and favour certain books over others. So worry not, but apply anyway. If you get on these sites you could see a HUGE, COLOSSAL amount of downloads.

Authormarketingclub.com is an invaluable resource for writers and self-publishers, it does cost, but it's well worth the $149. It has places to submit your books to, advice and loads of other great stuff. You should check it out.

Anything else than the above is kind of pointless and time wasting — some writers love to talk about FaceBook and Twitter, well NO! Not here… let me burst a bubble — they are a waste of time. When did you ever buy something that was advertised on FaceBook or Twitter? Or even just shared by someone? Me, never ever.

What I'd suggest is if you want to learn all about Kindle marketing, is go look on Amazon for a specific book about it. The best advice and marketing strategy that I know is this… write more books. Also, if you want to know how to do a KDP free giveaway, which you should, then there are some excellent books on the Kindle store that can walk you through it.

8.

Things you shouldn't do

Want to know something else that leaves me cold?

People who say it's essential that you have a website, otherwise called an "author platform". Ergh, it makes me cringe. Seriously, what is the point?

There are some great stats in Michael Alvear's book "Make a Killing on Kindle" in which he actually looks at whether a blog or website is necessary. The results are pretty conclusive — having a blog gets you a ridiculously low percentage of sales. And think about the time it takes to set up a blog and get it running and write all the content for it and make it successful and rank on Google and all that mind numbing crap — just to sell a couple of books a month.

Sorry, bubble bursting time again — it's not worth it. Save yourself the chore. This is me saving you countless hours of your precious time. These hours that you spend on your blog could be spent writing another book and making yourself more money. I cannot say it any clearer or louder, blogs are a waste of time.

Yes it may have worked for them and they can fill a couple of chapters on it, but I'm here to tell you to be patient and wait. If your dream is to have a blog or internet presence, then get yourself a book that tells you how to do that. You don't need a blog to build an eBook Empire, simple.

Here is my advice. Forget about blogs for now. Do this instead: when you have 10 books out on Amazon, that's when you should make a website, call it your author name and have all your books on there with links to Amazon. Keep it simple, maybe put an email sign up form on there too. No blogging, just a website.

The same goes for a mailing list:

You can set up a simple mailing list form on <u>MailChimp.com</u> that runs via a FaceBook page. This is a good idea and quick to set up. You can pay someone to set up a FaceBook page for you too. But again, only when you have lots of books out, otherwise you're wasting time.

I can't remember the last time I clicked on someone's sign up form at the back of a book, and I don't know who would. Some people must otherwise these writers wouldn't do it. So it must be worthwhile. However, just wait until you're an authority.

Me personally? I still haven't got round to it, and I have loads of books out.

You know it makes sense right?

You may be wondering why I am telling you all this, I could just keep it all secret and let people waste their time on blogs and mailing lists that do little to build their empire. Well, I am an empathetic person who believes that instead of trying to trick newbies to the self-publishing world that they should be encouraged. Competition is healthy. Very healthy. The more quality on Kindle, the more people that buy on Kindle and if they buy your book they might stumble across mine too and then everyone is a winner.

Like I mentioned earlier, at some point in the building of your empire, the time will be right to start to build these things. A mailing list first, followed by a website.

When that time comes, just download a Kindle book about how to do it and work on it. Or pay someone to do it for you.

The main reason I say all this is that this world is hard and there are so many distractions. When I started out, I read Kindle book after Kindle book about how to self-publish, they all said the same. But what I was doing was just prolonging in starting my empire. Stop delaying.

Making an email list is useful when you are selling enough books, but when you only have one book out? Pointless.

The object of this book is to tell you not to waste your time. Getting a ghostwriter is about saving yourself time. So why waste all that time in pointless things?

9.

Multiple steams of income

Turning your books into multiple streams of income:

So, your book(s) is/are published on Amazon and you're making a steady income. Here are some ideas that don't take long like the other things I think I made my point with, but can and will bring in some much needed extra dough. They also make you more of an authority.

On your Kindle book page, what looks better? Having just a Kindle version of your book for sale. Or having a paperback, hardback and an audiobook?

If you don't know, it's the latter. Having more options available to buyers makes you... more money! It also looks a lot better, because Amazon tells the customer how much they save by buying the Kindle version against the paperback.

So I've already mentioned a couple of things, let me elucidate:

Audiobooks:

I will be publishing a complete guide very shortly about how and why you should be making an audiobook of your Kindle eBook. I think this is a growing market. Amazon's Audible service has been left by the wayside a little by Amazon but it won't be long until they reinvent it and the audiobook, and I want to be involved when that happens. But even now Amazon makes it incredibly easy to get your audiobook out there. With the ACX program, you can simply type in the name of your book, lay claim to it, saying that you are the author. Then, you can choose to upload the audiobook that you recorded, or choose to be partnered with a narrator/producer who will make the audiobook for you and take a percentage of the sales.

It costs nothing to do this and you can add a great amount of royalties. Amazon also offers a bounty programme so if someone signs up to Audible and makes your book their first download then you get a $25 bounty bonus!

Youtube:

What I then do, following on from the piracy principle, is upload the audiobook I recorded on Audible, to Youtube. "Why?" I hear you say. Because if it's on Youtube, with a description linking it to Amazon, then more people can see it and buy it. I release each chapter as a separate video on Youtube, then the whole thing as a separate video. I make the book cover as the video too. You can make all this really easily on a free video editor, just put the picture of the cover in the video line and the audiobook in the audio line. Then fill in all the other info or fancy bits you can think of.

Paperbacks:

This is a great idea for fiction authors. Some people still prefer hard copies and you should make it available. It can be a faff to get one formatted and sorted. Unless you're familiar with Adobe Illustrator, it can take a long time. Added to that the fact you have to do a completely new cover with a spine and all sorts, it can be exhausting. I suggest outsourcing the entire thing to someone to do it for you and then go through the CreateSpace.com program. Amazon automatically puts your paperback and Kindle book together on the same page.

You won't make much from the paperback, maybe 10% of your Kindle sales, but that's still an extra 10%!

Again, I will be writing another book walking you through how to do this in the near future.

Hardcover:

Kind of pointless in all honesty. But if you want one for your ego, go ahead. Some people really like them. CreateSpace doesn't do them, but lightningsource.com does. I've never done it but I sure will some time in the future just to expand the brand.

There are opportunities to explore many other avenues. If you have a non-fiction book that would make a great course, then have a look at udemy.com, or clickbank.com. There are so many opportunities and it all changes so quickly. However, I would advise not to get too involved in anything else much from the above.

So let's get excited again…

I have some more numbers for you that should make you extra excited about embarking on this journey together. I did them this morning in my notebook as I thought about the finances of this thing and how long it would take to earn our money back when we ghostwrite.

If I was starting out, this is what I'd do…

Save up about $50 a week, or £32.50 in the UK and put it into my special work account. I then go on oDesk and hire a freelance writer for $100 for a book writing project — fiction or non-fiction, it doesn't matter.

I do this every fortnight. So in those two weeks, I've saved the $100 or £65. This way I can get two books a month written for $200 or £120.

Obviously, there are other costs like getting a cover, formatting, etc… that we've already discussed. But for now let's use the actual writing of the thing our benchmark.

After 10 months, we have 20 books out and have spent $1,200 or £650 on the writing. This could be 3 fiction series, or a couple of non-fiction niche series, or 20 stand-alone books.

Now let's start conservatively:

If we made the minimum on every book, so 99c or 99p, that's 30c/p royalty. Let's say we sell one of each book a day, that's a good conservative amount, especially for a series.

0.3 x 20 = $6 a day

$6 x 7 days in a week is $42p/w.

Per month, that's $168. Doesn't sound a lot right, but…

After 10 months? We have $1680!

So we spent $1200. And we've made $1680. That's profit, on the most conservative estimate and lowest royalty.

Wow!

Now let's imagine we have them all bundled up and into

funnels. The average royalty on a 7 book funnel selling at $9.99 is about $7.

Let's say we sell one bundle each a day. That's $21 x 7 =147. Per month is $588.

And times by 10 = $5,880! A huge profit!

What I would actually do is use most of that profit to reinvest and get more eBooks written.

10.

Recap: the Formula

So this is a quick recap of my formula which you can copy and repeat yourself. Just make sure you send credit where credit is due when you're raking it in ;)

1. Decide upon non-fiction or fiction for your first book or series.

2. Plan the series

3. Plan your first book

4. Write it / get it ghostwritten

5. Edit it / get it edited

6. Make a cover / get a cover made

7. Do keywords, categories and book description

8. Upload to KDP

9. Market the book, use Fiverr gigs / upload to free book sites

10. Do a KDP select book giveaway

11. Make an audiobook and paperback

12. Repeat!

Simple, huh?

Conclusion:

So there we have it, your complete guide to coming up with a great idea for some books, writing or getting them ghostwritten and building up what could be a huge monthly income, if you do it right and produce quality that people want to read.

Now, this is the first book that I am writing and publishing myself about self-publishing.

I will be writing lots more, exploring some of the subjects I've discussed already such as: *writing the books yourself, making Kindle eBook covers, making audiobooks,* and even a: *complete guide to self-publishing for beginners,* where I walk you through uploading to Kindle.

But until next time, it's been a pleasure to write this and I look forward to hearing from you.

11.

Recommended reading

Here I include most of the books that I read when I starting my empire. Some are better than others. People think I am crazy for including the books of my '*rivals*', but I don't see it that way — as I said, credit where credit is due.

Thank you to all of the writers of these books:

Write, Publish, Repeat, by Sean Platt and Johnny B. Truant

Writing a Novel with Scrivener, by David Hewson

2k to 10k, by Rachel Aaron

The Kindle Publishing Bible, by Tom Corson-Knowles

Let's Get Digital, by David Gaughran

Make a Killing on Kindle, by Michael Alvear

Earn More, Work Less, Get Famous! by Simon Hodgkinson

Writing a Kindle Book a Week, by Alex Forster

There are lots of other great books, but these are the ones to start with.

Thank you for taking the time to read this. If you enjoyed it then I would be very grateful if you left a review on Amazon so that others may find it as well.

Yours,

Arthur Dylan

www.ingramcontent.com/pod-product-compliance
Lightning Source LLC
Chambersburg PA
CBHW030524290526
45786CB00004B/1617